le hammond

... a handy beginner's guide!

Published by **Wise Publications**

Exclusive Distributors: Music Sales Limited,
14-15 Berners Street, London W1T 3LJ, UK

Order No. AM1008425
ISBN 978-1-78305-457-2

This book © Copyright 2014 Wise Publications.

Edited by Ruth Power.
Inside layout by Fresh Lemon.

Made in China.

Unauthorised reproduction of any part of this
publication by any means including photocopying
is an infringement of copyright.

www.musicsales.com

54 Trill
55 Wah
56 Crying
57 The Crying Blues
60 Vibrato
61 Tremolo
62 Tongued notes
63 Improvising
65 City Blues Jam
68 Midnight Blues Jam
70 Harp Legends: Sonny Boy Williamson II
72 Glossary
76 Recommended listening
78 What you've learnt

What type of harmonica?

There are many different types of harmonicas available, in many different keys. The best suited for a beginner is the C harmonica, also known as the C 'harp'. It has a single row of 10 holes and is marked with the letter C.

Parts of the harp

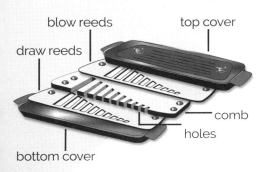

Hold your harp

Hold the harmonica as shown in the picture. You can hold with either hand as long as you have a firm grip on the harmonica and can use the other hand at the back to cup the sound.

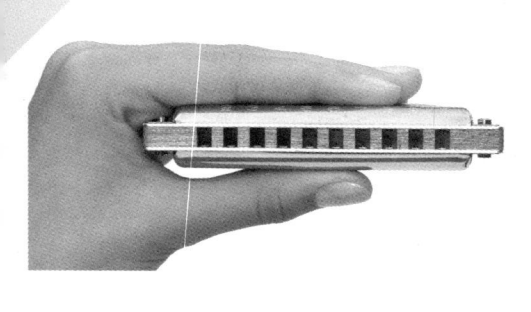

The cupping hand

Cup the back of the harmonica as shown in the picture. This hand is important for creating different sound effects later on.

Getting started

Hold the harmonica with the low notes on the left. If your harmonica has numbers, the '1' should be on the left.

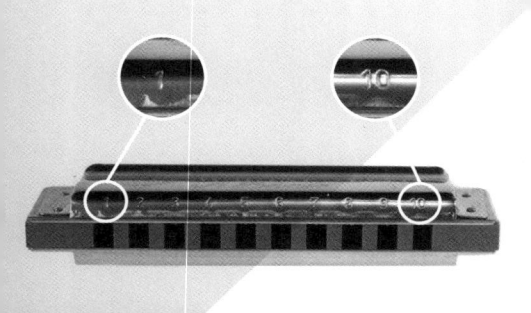

Your first chord

Put your mouth over holes 3, 4 and 5 and suck gently. You are playing a group of notes (called a **chord**) which we call G[7]. The jarring sound of the 4 and 5 holes played together is the heart of the blues. The 5 hole is the blue note.

High and low

Try blowing and sucking up and down the harp, getting a feel for the difference in the pitches and the amount of breath needed for higher or lower notes.

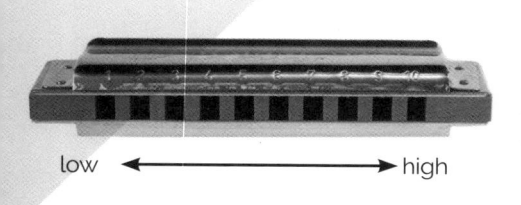

low ←————————————→ high

Make sure you move the harp using your hands, not by moving your head, or you will become tired quickly. This will ensure better accuracy when aiming for certain notes.

Breathing

You need to breathe deeply through your lungs and not just suck and push air through your lips. The proper term for suck is to **draw**, because you draw the breath from down inside you. The work should be done by the diaphragm not from the chest. If you simply use your cheeks and lips you will get tired quickly.

You may find it helps to imagine the sound you are producing as like a ping-pong ball supported on the column of air coming from your lungs, and if you blow too hard the ball will fall.

Try not to tense up too much; just breathe in and out through the instrument and stay relaxed.

Breathing tips

The less air you can use, the better –
and the longer your note will last!

Always remember to move the harmonica across your mouth – don't move your head – it's far less accurate. If you think you're having trouble with this, try practising in front of a mirror.

Stay relaxed and let your breathing be deep, free and easy. Try to produce single notes clearly without interference from neighbouring holes and without the 'fuzziness' that can sneak in.

Tab symbols

In order to learn the music in this playbook you will need to read the following tablature symbols (called '**TAB**' for short). These symbols will tell you what to play. Here are the TAB symbols you will need to learn:

▲ The up arrow indicates a **blow** note.

▼ The down arrow indicates a **draw** note.

⧨ The double arrows are bent notes, which we will learn about later.

⧩ The up and down double arrows are **bends** down and back up again.

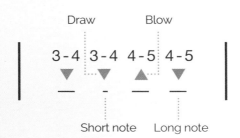

The lines underneath the arrows indicate long notes (like this —) and short notes (like this -). The tab is divided into sections called bars. There is a set number of beats to count in each bar. For this Playbook we will mostly be counting four beats to the bar. Each beat is indicated with this symbol: ●

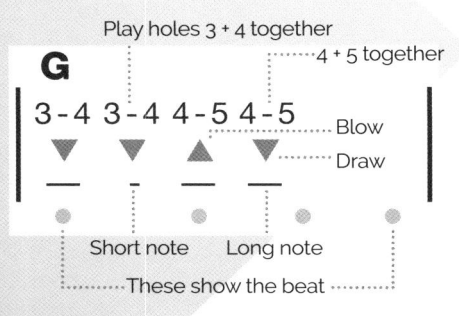

Play holes 3 + 4 together

4 + 5 together

G

3 - 4   3 - 4   4 - 5   4 - 5   — Blow

▼   ▼   ▲   ▼   ····· Draw

Short note   Long note

These show the beat

Along the top of the TAB are capital letters to indicate the chord to be played with the tune. If you have someone to accompany you on another instrument they can use the chords indicated to play along. If not, you can simply ignore these letters.

Keeping the beat

A beat is the natural tapping rhythm of a song – when you tap your foot to a piece of music you are responding to the beat. In order to keep the beat consistent music is divided into small sections called '**bars**' (or '**measures**').

Each bar has a fixed number of beats in it. Most tunes have four beats in a bar, so you would count and/or tap your foot 1, 2, 3, 4. Some tunes will have only three beats to a bar, so you would count 1, 2, 3. This is often referred to as a '**waltz**'.

Single notes

Playing one single note instead of several requires a smaller shape of your mouth. Try pursing your lips around the harmonica until you find a shape that is comfortable to play a single note.

Try playing the note C by blowing on the 4th hole. Be careful to only sound that note and not let other notes sneak in.

4.

Bonnie's Waltz

You may recognise this tune as 'My Bonnie Lies Over The Ocean'. It is an exercise in ¾ time, or waltz time. We count 1 2 3 to each bar.

This waltz introduces some higher notes to your playing which will require some careful breathing. You need a little more pressure to get a clean note, but be careful not to over-blow .

Key: C
Time: 3/4
Feel: Folky

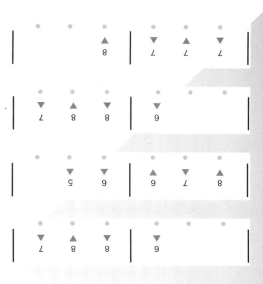

This final barline indicates the end of the song.

Notes by number

Here is a diagram to show the names of the notes created when each hole on the C harmonica is sounded through either blowing, or drawing on it.

Blow

C E G C E G C E G C

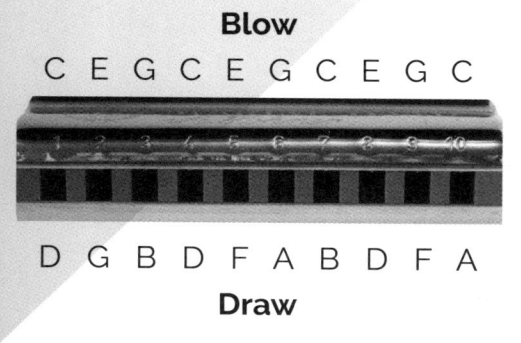

D G B D F A B D F A

Draw

C major chord

At the beginning you learned to play a G⁷ chord by drawing on holes 3, 4 and 5. The second chord to learn is a C major chord, played by blowing holes 1, 2 and 3 together. To do this you'll need to widen the shape of your mouth to include the three holes.

This sounds the notes C, E and G, creating a cheerful sounding chord.

Skip To My Lou

This classic tune requires you to play pairs of notes – slightly easier than one at a time. Aim for clarity with each pair and avoid slurring between each pair as you move the instrument. To play the quicker notes try going "duh," with your tongue to make them all distinct.

Key: C
Time: 4/4
Feel: Country/bouncy

| 4-5 | 4-5 | 3-4 | 3-4 | | 4-5 | 4-5 | 5-6 |
| ▲ | ▲ | ▲ | ▲ | | ▲ | ▲ | |

| 3-4 | 3-4 | 2-3 | 2-3 | | 3-4 | 3-4 | 4-5 |
| ▼ | ▼ | ▼ | ▼ | | ▼ | ▼ | ▼ |

| 4-5 | 4-5 | 3-4 | 3-4 | | 4-5 | 4-5 | 5-6 |
| ▲ | ▲ | ▲ | ▲ | | ▲ | ▲ | ▲ |

| 3-4 | 3-4 | 4-5 | 3-4 | | 3-4 | | 3-4 |
| ▼ | ▼ | ▲ | ▼ | | ▲ | | ▲ |

HARP LEGENDS

Bob Dylan

Many a purist may wince when they hear the rough and ready sound of **Bob Dylan** playing the harmonica. No doubt Dylan will accept that he is no virtuoso. But then he never set out to be.

Dylan is the ultimate example of a harmonica as the extension of the human voice and its purity and directness of expression. His playing is the perfect complement to the power and evocative imagery of his lyrics and his guitar style.

Essential tracks:

'Just Like A Woman'
'Mr Tambourine Man'
'Tangled Up In Blue'

Arpeggio

Now you've learned the C **major chord** on holes 1, 2 and 3, we are going to use this chord and some more notes to create an **arpeggio**. With holes 1, 2 and 3 we already have the notes C, E and G respectively. If you move your lips to blow on hole four you will get another C higher in the scale.

Now practise moving the harmonica backwards and forwards between the four holes, playing the notes C, E, G, C, G, E, C. Try not to pause for a breath between the notes.

Before long, you should get a smooth sequence of notes up and down the scale, this is an arpeggio: the notes of the chord played individually in a sequence.

Next repeat exactly what you have just done, but this time drawing instead of blowing. This is a **G chord arpeggio**.

The Blues

The secret to blues harp playing is that you mainly use draw notes, rather than blow notes. To learn which draw notes to play in which context we need to look at some theory.

When we play a C harp we are playing in the key of C major, however this is very happy sounding and not at all bluesy. In order to make it sound bluesy we must play a form of a minor scale over the major chord.

Playing crossed position by drawing first then blowing, we can use G as the new root note. With the notes available on the C harp, this produces a type of minor scale with a flattened 7th note (the F) creating the blues feel.

G	A	B	C	D	E	F
1	2	3	4	5	6	♭7

Effectively you are playing a form of minor scale across a major key and it is the clash of semitones and tones that make for the blues effect.

The blues scale

The **blues scale** is not so different from this new crossed position scale. This is why we use it as a base to create more blue notes when needed.

By drawing on the C harp we can create a G blues scale:

G B♭ C D♭ D F

1 ♭3 4 ♭5 6 ♭7

The ♭3 and ♭5 aren't available naturally on the harp as the ♭7 is, but we can achieve these notes through bending down on the 3 and 5 notes. We'll learn about bending notes after we've played a simple blues tune.

HARP LEGENDS

Sonny Terry

Before it got to Chicago and became electrified, the harmonica was one of the standard instruments of the country blues men. It was cheap, readily available and easy to play.

For people like **Sonny Terry**, who was handicapped by blindness as well as his status as a black man in the American South, it provided a rare passport to world-wide fame.

His bouncy, rhythmic style is firmly rooted in his country roots and he is also the definitive exponent of special harmonica effects like the 'chugging train', the 'wailing whistle' and the 'hounds chasing the fox'.

At times, the calls of his voice and the responses he plays on the harmonica are almost indistinguishable.

Essential tracks:
'Louise, Louise'
'Whoopin' The Blues'

The Two-timing Blues

Here is a tune for you to try; this is in the key of G, and counts four beats to the bar. It uses only holes 2-6 and a mixture of blowing and drawing notes. On the quicker notes use your tongue to stop the sound instead of stopping with your breath.

Key: G
Time: 4/4
Feel: Gentle shuffle

G

3-4 3-4 4-5 4-5

▼ ▼ ▲ ▼

— - — —

G

3-4 3-4 4-5 4-5

▼ ▼ ▲ ▼

— - — —

G

3-4 3-4 4-5 4-5

▼ ▼ ▲ ▼

— - — —

G

3-4 3-4 4-5 4-5

▼ ▼ ▲ ▼

— - — —

C7

4-5 4-5 4-5 5-6

▲ ▲ ▼ ▲

— - — —

C7

4-5 4-5 4-5 5-6

▲ ▲ ▼ ▲

— - — —

C harps

C harps are marketed under a variety of names such as Bluesmaster, Meisterklasse, Pocket Pal, Easy Rider, Blues Harp, Lee Oskar and many more.

Bending

If you listen to the great harp players, you will hear the harmonica wailing and crying as they play. These sounds are usually made by bending the reed inside the harmonica with your breath. It's not that difficult, but it's one of the hardest things you will have to learn, so let's get it out of the way now.

This is the symbol that indicates you should bend the note.

You have been blowing a single note on the fourth hole. To start wailing, try drawing a single note on the fourth hole. It's the note of D. To bend the note you have to change the shape of your mouth and tongue, so that the air comes through the harp in a different way.

Try curling the back of your tongue up towards the back of your mouth; your lower jaw might move forward a bit at the same time, which is fine. You'll need to draw a little harder; remember to breathe deep. Keep changing the shape of your mouth until you hear the note begin to drop.

Wailing

You have already learned to bend a note. Wailing on the harmonica uses the same technique. Practise gently bending and unbending the note. Played in one movement, bending and unbending the note creates a wailing effect.

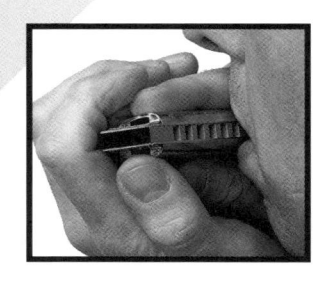

One-note Wail

Here's a second tune which includes a one-note wail. At the end of the tune is a symbol which instructs you to go back to the beginning and play the song again.

Key: G
Time: 4/4
Feel: Medium country style

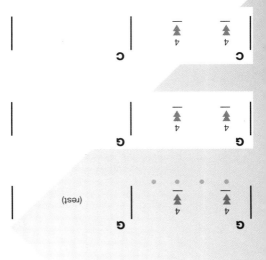

This repeat sign tells you to play again from the begininning.

HARP LEGENDS

Little Walter

Walter Jacobs, known as **Little Walter** because he was so young when he first broke upon the Chicago blues scene, is the king of the amplified harmonica style. He was a sonic innovator, willing to use the effects and processes that were being developed in the recording studios of the Forties and Fifties to add an extra dimension to his sound.

On tracks like 'Blue Light' you can hear him revelling in the harmonics that he coaxes from the combination of his booming harmonica and the reverb chamber. He also made extensive use of the chromatic harmonica.

Essential tracks:
'Juke'
'Blue Light'
'I Just Want To Make Love To You'
(with Muddy Waters)
'Louisiana Blues'
(with Muddy Waters)

More about chords

If you play more than one note at the same time, you're playing a chord. We've already used chords in playing the 'Two-timing Blues' earlier, but we're going to look at them in a bit more detail now because they are useful for adding dynamics and style to your playing, and are essential for accompaniment.

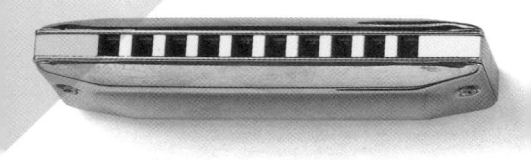

Rather than learn every type of chord you can play, we are going to focus on playing the main chords used on a C harp, those based on C and G. We will look at some ways to make accompaniment and solos more interesting by creating effects with those chords.

The harmonica is a unique instrument because the mouth and hands contribute most of the sound. They form a sound chamber that when moved in different ways can subtly or dramatically alter the sound. The following effects are created by moving the mouth and/or hands around in different ways.

Trill

Another harp effect to learn is the trill. This is another basic harp effect that features in countless urban and rural blues performances.

Move the harp quickly from side to side in your mouth, so that two holes next to each other alternate. Be careful to get a good clean trilling sound. Sound the notes clearly and don't let other notes sneak in.

Wah

To create the wah sound, start by drawing on hole 4, opening and closing your cupping hand. The more airtight the chamber when your hand is closed, the better the effect will be.

Crying

To really make the harp wail and cry we can use a combination of the wah and wail. Try bending the note up and down as you move your cupping hand, altering the speed of your hand. Practise with other holes, some chords and then have a go at the following tune.

The Crying Blues

This alternates long slow wahs and long fast wahs on one or two notes at a time.

Key: G
Time: 4/4
Feel: Slow blues

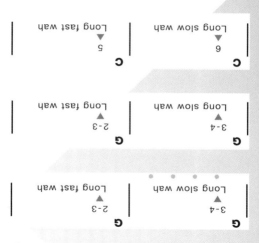

Vibrato

The key point to make about vibrato in particular is not to over use it. If every note is wobbling, it quickly becomes irritating to listen to, and the effect is wasted.

Vibrato is a form of bend, but it involves the tip of the tongue rather than the back. Essentially you need to say "yuh-yuh-yuh" as you draw or blow a note.

Tremolo

Tremolo is a real test of your breathing technique, because it has to come from right down in your abdomen. Draw your breath in little jerks; try going "uh-uh-uh" right at the back of your throat, and further down, if you can.

You should feel it in your stomach muscles to get the real depth of emotional impact.

Tongued notes

To add attack, or create a staccato effect, go "dah" with the tip of your tongue against the roof of your mouth.

This technique gives extra clarity and emphasis to each note or chord. Use it freely between the smooth draws and blows to create contrast and extra rhythmic punch.

Improvising

Improvising requires the use of your ears more than ever. You have to listen to the music and make sure your playing fits with the tune or chords being played and you also have to know when to keep quiet.

The magic of improvisation is that the further you get from the tune, the more exciting the music becomes.

The only way to learn the craft of improvisation is to practise it. Start by using the techniques you've learned here, then start copying some of the techniques you hear when listening to great harmonica players. Then you can add your own ideas.

Make sure you play in a group with other musicians; this is where you will really adapt your style, and learn how to think on your feet.

Now that you have learnt the basics here are some tunes for you to cut your teeth on. These are relatively simple so that you can begin to experiment with improvising.

City Blues Jam

This song starts with just one beat before we begin counting full bars. This is called a **pick-up**. Think of it as beginning on 4 like this: **4, 1, 2, 3, 4...**

Key: G
Time: 4/4
Feel: Quick shuffle

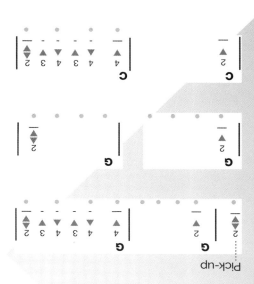

Midnight Blues Jam

This song is in a new key, D minor. Draw on the fourth hole for the root note.

Key: Dm
Time: 4/4
Feel: Slow, dark blues

Dm6

$\hat{4}$
▲
•

Dm6

4   5   4   3
▲   ▼   ▲   ▲
•   •   •   •

Gm6

6   5   5   5
▼   ▼   ▲   ▼
–   –   –   •
•   •

Dm6

4
▲
(rest)

Gm6

6	5	5	3	2
▲	▼	▲	▼	▼

Gm6

6	5	5	4	2
▲	▼	▲	▼	▼

Dm6

3
▼

Dm6

4	5	4
▼	▲	▼

Am6

5	5	4	5	4
▼	▲	▼	▲	▼

Gm6

6	5	5	4	5	3
▲	▼	▲	▼	▲	▼

Dm6   **Gm6**

2	3	4	4	5	6
▼	▼	▼	▲	▲	▲

Am6

6	5	4
▲	▼	▼

69

HARP LEGENDS

Sonny Boy Williamson II

For many, **Sonny Boy** (born Rice Miller) is the daddy of all harp players. Argument still rages over whether he was the original Sonny Boy Williamson, or was simply trying to cash-in on the success of John Lee, but there is no doubting the unique quality and power of his playing. Like Count Basie, he manages to invest more power and emotive expression in a single note than can be found in the cascades of notes from less gifted artists.

His sound is instantly recognisable and his voice, as it laces his lazy poetry between the riffs, evokes whisky, women and the very essence of the blues with compelling ease.

Essential tracks:
'Mighty Long Time'
'Help Me'
'Bring It On Home'

Glossary

Bars – a segment of time defined by a certain number of beats or counts.

Bends – where a note is bent (much like how a guitar bends a string to create a different note) by adjusting the position of the mouth.

Blues note – there are three notes that are particular to the blues scale, the ♭3, ♭5 and ♭7.

Chord – when more than one note is sounded at the same time this creates a chord. Some of the more popular combinations of notes have a chord name like major or minor.

Cross harp – a blues technique (also known as second position) where drawing on the harp instead of blowing sounds in the key one fifth above the natural tuning.

Crying – creating an emotive sound by bending the note or notes.

Cup – curving the hand over the back of the harmonica to shape the sound.

Diatonic – the natural key.

Draw – to breathe inward through the harmonica, also known as sucking.

Dynamics – the loud and quiet moments in music.

First position – playing in the natural key by blowing and drawing.

Improvisation – to play from your own ideas, in keeping with the song structure and harmony.

Key – indicates the home chord or note which gives a sense of final resting for the piece.

Major chord – a group of notes when sounded gives a sense of happiness, using the tones 1, 3, 5 of the scale.

Minor chord – a group of notes when sounded gives a sense of sadness, using the tones 1, ♭3, 5 of the scale.

Scale – a set of notes played in order of pitch.

Reed – little strips of metal attached to a metal plate which is fixed onto the body of the harp, over the holes. The sound of the harmonica is made by the reeds vibrating in the air, classifying it as a free reed instrument

Riffing – a derivative of the word 'refrain' which means a repeated verse or note pattern, a riff is a note pattern that is popular within its style.

Root – the home note of the key.

More on the harp

To learn more about playing the harmonica and learn more songs, try these titles:

- **The Complete Harmonica Player** (AM997449)
- **The Beatles Harmonica Songbook** (NO90549)
- **Starting Blues Harmonica** (AM991342)

MORE IN THE playbook SERIES

available from all good music shops or, in case of difficulty contact: music@musicsales.co.uk

Introduction

This playbook will get you playing the harmonica in no time! You'll learn the basic techniques you need as well as fun effects to add character to your playing.

Let's get started!

Contents

6 What type of
harmonica?

7 Parts of the harp

8 Hold your harp

9 The cupping hand

10 Getting started

11 The first chord

12 High and low

14 Breathing

16 Breathing tips

18 Tab symbols

21 Keeping the beat

22 Single notes

23 Bonnie's Waltz

26 Notes by number

27 C major chord

28 Skip To My Lou

30 Harp legends:
Bob Dylan

32 Arpeggio

34 The Blues

36 The blues scale

38 Harp Legends:
Sonny Terry

40 The Two-timing
Blues

43 C Harps

44 Bending

46 Wailing

47 One-note Wail

50 Harp Legends:
Little Walter

52 More about
chords

Second position – playing one fifth above the natural key (see Cross harp).

Tongue stopping – use the tongue to block the airflow through the hole, this is used for playing quick notes.

Tremolo – a very quick stuttering of the note or notes.

Trill – where two notes (or sometimes more) are alternated quickly to create a fluttering effect.

Vibrato – quickly altering the pitch of a note creating a warbling effect.

Recommended listening

Now that you've got to grips with the fundamentals of harmonica playing, try listening to how the professionals do it!

The songs listed below all feature classic harmonica parts; some are more difficult than others, but armed with the basic techniques you've learnt in this playbook, you should soon be able to approach some of them.

'Good Morning Little School Girl'
John Mayall
'Love Me Do' The Beatles
'Magic Bus' The Who
'Midnight Rambler' The Rolling Stones
'Mr Tambourine Man' Bob Dylan
'The River' Bruce Springsteen
'There Must Be An Angel'
Eurythmics (with Stevie Wonder)
'Heart of Gold' Neil Young

What you've learnt

In this playbook you have learnt:

- How to hold the harp and breathe efficiently
- To play single notes and chords
- To read basic TAB symbols
- To play an arpeggio
- The blues scale
- Effects to add interest to your playing including bending, wailing and crying.

Now you can take what you've learnt and play along to your favourite harmonica music.